After the Firestorm

After the Firestorm

poems by Susan Kolodny

Mayapple Press 2011

Published by   MAYAPPLE PRESS
                      362 Chestnut Hill Rd.
                      Woodstock, NY 12498
                      www.mayapplepress.com

ISBN 978-1-936419-07-4

ACKNOWLEDGMENTS

There are many to whom I am grateful. A few of these have my especially deep and enduring gratitude because of their support for and interest in my writing. With my thanks, then, to Dan Chasman, for that red pencil; to Brooks Haxton, Brigit Pegeen Kelly, Ira Sadoff, and in memory of Renate Wood, for their generosity and help with this manuscript; to Brenda Hillman for her ongoing belief in and insights into my work; to dear poet friends Carol Snow, Forrest Hamer, Alice Jones, and Robert Thomas; to the Wally Tribe, who are my other home; and to Henry Markman, Ilse Jawetz, my husband Lewis Finneburgh and son Noah Finneburgh for having deepened and enriched my life. Thanks, also, to C. Dale Young for his astute editorial advice and to Judith Kerman, an excellent editor.

The author gratefully acknowledges the editors of the following journals in which versions of these poems first appeared:
88: A Journal of Contemporary Poetry, Bellingham Review, Beloit Poetry Journal, Black Warrior Review, Calyx, Cimarron Review, Embers, Green Mountains Review, HazMat Review, Mississippi Valley Review, New England Review, River Styx, Salt Hill, Sow's Ear, ThreePenny Review.

The author is grateful also to the following anthologies in which these poems appeared:
Anthology of Magazine Verse and Yearbook of American Poetry, 1997, Verse and Universe: Poems about Science and Mathematics, Outsiders: Poems about Rebels, Exiles, and Renegades, A Fine Excess: Fifty Years of the Beloit Poetry Journal, The Place That Inhabits Us: Poems of the San Francisco Bay Watershed.

Cover photo by Wong YooChong. Cover designed by Judith Kerman. Book designed and typeset by Amee Schmidt with titles in Bradley Hand ITC and text in Californian FB. Author photo courtesy of Lewis Finneburgh.

Contents

I.

II.

III.

For my teachers

I.

Lagoon

In all the universe, there is one sound.
It beats in my ears, muffled heart drum,
mine, amid the filtered, shimmering light.
Prone, over coral—its sulci and gyri,
its longing, arching, branching shapes,
a congregation praying—I float.
Among jewelfish that dart and glide—
opalescent silver, orange and melon green,
parabolas of color in space—among these shapes
I drift. Far from the shore, my link to human,
far from horizons that summon, fade, there is only color
as though some crayon-mad child had run amok,
or a flower bed exploded in deep space.

Near me, orange-and-black-striped sergeant-major fish
swarm past dense as bees. Pink, blue and green parrot fish.
There is a clearing. I float above the pink tentacles
of sea anemones, a host of flame-blue angel fish. . .
The black triangular back of a manta ray passes beneath me.
His tail, a slow lash, undulates. He somersaults,
revealing white belly, and somersaults:
a shadow along the white floor
of the turquoise and aqua sea.

Delusions of snorkel: I cross kingdoms,
no gravity, no seams. Far from fear,
the limitless safely limited by a ring of coral reef,
semipermeable membrane between land and sea,
between neon slivers of electric blue damsel fish,
and the savage things that larger lurk
beyond the barrier reef.

I look up. Some terror has swum through
a splintering breach. I am alone with it
in a place not human, in a place without air.
I am alone among fish and am not one:
Columbus drifting nearer the flat cliff

of the world. The muffled drum beats faster,
prismatic colors swirl, shadows invade
the lagoon floor, sunlight is sucked
into caves, sands beneath me darken. My body
wants to flee, but can only crawl towards shore.

Koi Pond

Our shadows bring them from the shadows:
a yolk-yellow one with a navy pattern
like a Japanese woodblock print of fish scales.
A fat, 18-karat one splashed with gaudy purple
and a patch of gray. One with a gold head,
a body skim-milk-white, trailing ventral fins
like half-unfolded fans of lace.
A poppy-red, slightly disheveled one,
and one, compact, all indigo in faint green water.
They wear comical whiskers and gather beneath us
as we lean on the cement railing
in indecisive late December light,
and because we do not feed them, they pass,
then they loop and circle back. Loop and circle. Loop.
"Look," you say, "beneath them." Beneath them,
like a subplot or a motive, is a school
of uniformly dark ones, smaller, unadorned,
perhaps another species, living in the shadow
of the gold, purple, yellow, indigo and white,
seeking the mired roots and dusky grasses,
unliveried, the quieter beneath the quiet.

Silk

The first silk thing
I ever wore
was a sleeveless
China-blue-chrysanthemum-on-white
block print, a summer dress
on loan from my mother—
an almost perfect fit.
Its full skirt floated
around me, petal
on a current.
Under nightblooming jasmine,
among lit orange
Japanese paper lanterns,
I stood kissing
and being kissed by Hector O,
nearly nineteen, and very smooth,
even our French teacher
snapped her chalk
and stammered around him,
and the mothers, whose cigarettes
he would light. Hector O,
the son of a diplomat, maker
of bilingual puns, and the reason,
although I never confessed,
that I had sat
through six weeks
of *le subjonctif* and failed
it, memorizing
the timbre of his voice,
the shadow of beard
on his cheek, and here we were,
plus que ça, on a spring night
in a garden, kissing
after his fingers brushed my wrist
at a party, kissing,

the silk rustling lushly,
whispering its warning,
lightly billowing
incense around me.

Close Relations

You come with me into my garden
where I show you
delicate, conventional roses
but not the insides of the snowdrops
with their green nimbus,
nor the thick, looping tree roots
like coiled serpents on the old maps
of *terra incognita*. Not
the secret folds of the peonies
preparing to open. You're in a hurry.
I show you only what I think you can see
and not how fragrant this soil is,
how aerated and wet with spring.
You think you've seen the garden.
You're satisfied, and we go now,
you not even suspecting
how pale the lichen are
on the white thighs of the birch tree,
or this bed that for three days in February
was purple with crocuses—*krokos*,
for saffron, aromatic spice
the innermost gold yields up,
which gold, also, you will not see.

Drought, Year 4

I knew we had had no rain
when the tents and hammocks
of the spiders, their white
rebozos, covered the front yard ivy,
antimacassars over the twigs
of the pear tree,
weavings among the wisteria tendrils,
many elaborate nets, some still joined
to their spinners as the women
in their huipiles
in Chichicastenango,
may still be seen weaving,
one end of the warp
around their waists, the other
around a tree trunk.
And even inside, strands
brush my arm or cheek. Spiders
with legs like beaded fringe,
at work in closet and cupboard, or suddenly,
in midair in front of us.
With no rain to wash them away,
the garden vanishes
under white quilts, gauze,
safety nets, trapezes,
fine gazebos, rhombs,
concave and convex veils,
our living, drought-resistant garden
shrouded in lace.

Love Poem

Your eyes are a city
I lived in once,
your voice the route
I took there, home.
I know your voice's turns,
the camber of its roads,
its precise places.
I know your silences'
shadows, varied as bells,
your pauses, where thought
collects from corners
it has scattered to
as children scatter, trusting
they'll be summoned home.
I know your inflections
as I know my rooms in darkness,
as the bat knows the cave
to which it flies.

Appreciating

Yesterday, I remembered
the lake we rowed on then.
Echo Lake.
Who'd have imagined
so ordinary an hour,
rowing at lunchtime
in the rented boat,
would become like
the only coin issued
with an inverted "d,"
unintended, making it
immeasurably valued—
the only or the last
of anything you don't know
until after will be.

Paros, View from the Harbor

This beauty is male,
but not a maleness that is
alien. It lacks violence.
It can wait.
It is, without needing
to impose or alter.
Like you,
this may change me
but doesn't insist
or even ask
that I change,
does not force
or obscure distinctions.
This beauty is white walls,
a red door, the light,
frank and impartial
on the docked blue fishing boat,
the whitewashed street,
the glass of water on the
round cafe table,
the vanished columns,
the yellow fishing nets
and wild sponges
drying on the beach.

Red

Ranunculus on your thin stem, surrounded
by buds that hang like Art Deco lamps,
like drooping heads, but slightly ominous, nearly
reptilian. Ranunculus with your black heart
and slightly ruffled petals, your leaves
long and jagged-edged, you go casually dressed,
unlike the rose, say, or the iris,
and have gotten yourself such fiery gypsy skirts.
See how fierce a red. On anyone else
it would be trashy, unseemly. On you, it is passion.
All night, I saw it in my sleep, that red,
saw it as I first did, encountering you almost at dusk
on the garden trail to the sea. I stopped, stared.
Ah, ranunculus, he isn't mine, but if I could wear that red,
I'd dance for him with castanets,
turning up such heat, we'd have to hurl ourselves—
So does that red simmer, steam, explode.

The Gift

I keep it on my desk—
the blown glass
stoppered perfume bottle
with its muted swirls
of seagreen, olive, mauve,
and hints of white and lime, flat
on the very bottom, then
a delicate egg, a slender neck,
a rolled, high glass collar,
and on top, the smooth
beret of the stopper.
The man who gave it to me
loved me once. For twenty years
after I refused him
while the other waited
in the next room,
he sent gifts: a glass bird
with a glass cherry in its beak
that I hung from the window
in every place I lived (it caught
the light and sent one sheer ray
into the center of the room),
a recording of torchy
songs I danced to
with others, and this
blown glass
with its eloquent mists,
elusive
as he imagined me.

Dutch Masters

When you were a student here in America
I told you your brother must be blind
if he thought that you weren't beautiful.
Then I visited, and met
the same teasing brother, Stefan, tall
and gray-eyed like you. Lithe.
I never told you how quickly
I forgave him, then trembled in his presence.
As when he came up behind me,
gathered my long hair, lifted it from my neck
to fasten a tiny undone button,
then slowly lowered it back in place.
I didn't move, scarcely breathed.
I know I felt the room arrest itself
and become infused with light.
As in the Vermeers he took me
to Amsterdam to see, promising
I'd prefer them even to the Rembrandts. I did,
and I do now—that unbiased gaze
which sanctifies each form. The shadows
kept in abeyance by the light.
And the woman only a Master
may so alter with his gaze, and fix,
neither to breathe nor to cease breathing.

Singing

Spring. Midnight.
The pear tree is flowering.
Alive, it says, in white letters.
The gnarled wisteria blooms
by the walk, its perfume
mixed also with lilac.
And in the gutters of the roof,
matted pine needles wet with rain.
Yes-yes, chirp the crickets,
though it is not summer,
captive crickets to feed
the child's pet lizard.
Yes-yes, sing the innocents,
thinking as crickets and not
food, who are crickets
and food. Go on, sing,
I tell them, sing.
Forget your fate
in the green jaws.
Forget the lizard
waiting in his house of glass.

II.

Vigil

Along the side of the house, buds
on the peony, the lilac green and sticky.
In the garden, the magnolia blooms pink,
white, and burgundy.
February's unaccustomed cold revived these,
but stunned the rest. The avocado, brown,
sags against the house. On the trellis,
a thousand dead moths of bougainvillea.
All month, I was up and down
the stairs, my nights
a dialectic of thermometers.
Now January is March. The gardener
hauls away the casualties.
Like small Eurydices, the crocuses,
which this year I turned too late to see,
have gone back into the earth.
I scrutinize my child for illness,
frightening him, scan
the dazed fuchsias for hints of green,
study the resurgence of the lilacs.
Do we risk more when we look
or when we look away?

Tsuneko

These doctors dissolve from one into another
and never grow old, men into women, larger
into smaller, they no longer have names.
They give you blue pills, flattened pellets
to inflate and stay above the flood on—
an island hillock, a bamboo raft at home.

They say come back the second of April the
eleventh of May. You nod, Tsuneko. You have nodded
here always never saying I do not understand.
A nod will release you out into the air
among the green gold blue and silver droppings
of glass birds with your pills, to return the day
they are gone, the glass tube hollow as reeds.

Once you nodded and a new one said Do you
understand me and you said No.
Tell me how I can help you understand me. What
do you call today? You say the eighth month the sixth day.
Come again then on the ninth month the third day.

This you do, up the stairs to the white room,
not touching the polished railing lest you stick there
as you did once to the wood you clutched
and did not unstick even when you crossed the ocean
with the dark enemy soldier to live in this place
and have children who would leave you coming no more
on your birthday as your mother has not come
since the sky burned the horses melted your brother
turned to chalk your father to stone.

Here is the doctor, Tsuneko. From your bag
you give her the rose the voices told you
to bring her. Her face is a pond you have dropped a pebble in.
She looks at you and sees you there. You *are* there.
Then the melted horses and cindered trees flicker

you say the Thank You the Goodbye you have learned to
and you go back out into the cold air the frozen light
the north-south street the square flat stones.

Neuroanatomy

The fog over the boulevard,
    a thick cerebral cortex.
      I enter its folds, its sulci and gyri,
        the canyons beneath me
    like ventricles. Dusk
        seeps from them like dark fluids.

*

On a stretched canvas,
8 brains neatly arranged.
Over each, a cartoon cloud
emptied of image or speech.
Whose brain was this
that I weigh in my hands,
heavy, dense as bread dough
but porous? We lift orange
stick and scalpel,
begin our dissection.

*

Memory is probably stored chemically,
    in the synapse,
      microscopic gap that is Lethe's antithesis.
        Molecules ferry across
      rivers of remembering,
    reversing Charon's way
      between axon and dendrite.

*

What we loved,
    where we have lived, lost
    in the layers of white.

*

Where the boulevard reaches
        the north gate,
    the fog is so thick:
memories encountered in my office,
    lives under shifting layers
        of opacity. Images,
    as when the sun rises
and a gray house, a white fence,
            the branches of an oak appear.
    Or on a foggy street, suddenly,
        a woman in a raincoat. . . .

*

Folded within the neocortex
    are the gray masses
        regulating impulse and feeling,
    as under the recent hills,
        tectonic plates and magma.
The dissection proceeds but not
        to the layers we dream from.

*

While it was whole,
        before we had peeled off
    the blood vessels and meninges,
            and prepared to invade the cortex,
        I held it up. Whose brain?
            peeled off the cranial nerves:
        olfactory, optic, oculomotor. . .
    to the tenth, the vagus,
            meaning wanderer.

*

There's a party in the lab.
Parts of the brain
are scattered on my lap, my jeans.

Smelling of formaldehyde,
we sing Happy Birthday,
eat cake, resume our dissection.

*

I plummet through the folds
        of the cortex—
    thought, poem, terrors
            and longings murmured in my office:
electrical charges across the membranes
        between inside and out.

*

The professor, a woman, says,
"The *massa intermedia*,
one of the nerve bundles that join
the left and right hemispheres,
is absent at autopsy from 85%
of the male cadavers,
and 15% of the female cadavers.
Nothing whatsoever is known
    of its function, no funding
            to solve the mystery of what it does."

Over our dissecting trays,
    the women laugh, the men
            look bewildered.

*

Where fog is as thick as fatty sheaths
of myelin over axons,
I go deeper in. How different from maps,
from procedures by daylight—
the studied structures, unrecognizable.
Of what use, atlases of anatomy

when what in the text seemed merely complex
turns out to have neighboring and overlapping structures,
idiosyncratic convolutions,
no color codes or cardboard flags with names?

*

In the lab, the intricate mass
    we lift from its bucket
        and cheesecloth, menaces.
  So later the road
     will turn odd
  under the slant shadows
of what I'd imagined
    to be merely eucalyptus and pine.

Psychiatry's Wife

At night the sorrows
        sift, diagnoses rearrange
    themselves,
    green ascends, black
            fine-powders everything
you hear yesterday's speech
        like gears, a distant
        braying. Who goes into the kitchen
        and bakes bread at 3 a.m.?
Whose yesterday skinned its knees?
    I am sick to death of voices—
        mine, yours, his.
                Incessant. Plaintive.
    Begging to come in. Alms
        for the poor.
    You cannot help. When I went
        to Paris. When I go
    to Paris. When we made
        Play Doh in winter, the light
    was so thin that it seemed
            sickly. The voices
            everywhere apparent, heir
    apparent. Listen!
I am sick of having
        to listen. Gregorian chants, yes.
    The 3 perfect notes, a chord,
that trembled in the air that afternoon
        in the Baptistry at Pisa.
    Ringed all around by marble—
who is the dead bride
        memorialized in stone?—
            we shivered at the platinum purity
    of the sound. The human
        voice made flute, purified
                of report, retort, complaint.
    I am tired now
        of listening, more, tell me
    more. Prey, tell.

Comfort me, oh comfort me.
   Listen. He told me stories
      once, Uncle Wiggly; he was 9,
     I was 6 or 7.
   The voice disappeared into an alleyway,
     a narrow door, begged me to follow.

Sirens

Once my little sister, waist deep
in the Pacific, the day luminous,
took off her ruby ring.
The sea must have asked for it
in that voice in which such gifts
are asked of us.
"I dropped it," she screamed,
 and shut her ears to that voice.

*

I find you late at night, alone
on deck. You lean out over
the railing. You grow somber,
studying the water. What toll
does it ask? What must you
now yield to it, or refuse?

*

Two thousand feet above the Pacific,
I pause between breadfruit and plumeria,
a foot from the edge. The ocean seems
to be singing. It's me the water wants.
Lacking Odysseus' men, or the mast
to cling to, I sit down, lower my head,
listen to what one dare not, wrap
my arms around my legs like ropes.

Improbable Angels

Lucinda draws angels for me with crayons,
then devils offering candy. She rips
the drawings up. We tape them together,
I study them with her. "They're awful," she says.
"I'm awful. What I make is awful."

Lucinda says that at nine, she played games
with her grandpa, secret games he'd played
with her nine-year-old mother. For her ninth birthday,
Lucinda's brash, flame-haired mother, her pale,
amoeboid father, left her for two weeks alone
with grandpa in his trailer.

Lucinda draws me a tight cell of panic
with bars that oscillate and heat to molten,
a floor stark and cold. No ceiling.
There angels visit her, improbable angels who fall,
becoming dust at her feet. Next drawings,
they gain strength and stand up.
The cell of panic develops its corners of refuge.

Lucinda's mother learns I will be here not
for the usual one year, but for three,
and fears she'll lose her child, because Lucinda,
who has real red hair, is twelve,
is fat, has shed five pounds, talked back,
and begun to wash her hair.

Lucinda says this is the last time
she can come here. The hour nearly over,
she pulls her chair close and whispers,
in a voice of wet fur, "Keep my drawings
for me? Keep them forever?" She pulls closer.
I feel her breath on my cheek.
"I draw sometimes at home now. I think of you

and draw pictures. I wait for the angels.
Will you remember me?"

I look at the white cinderblock walls of the room,
a cube without windows, a safe box, then
think beyond it because unlike Lucinda, I can,
to the city hooded in fog, to the Bay,
where I am certain a small boat is sinking
in the indifferent water.

Word Pond

Go back, past the curtain of details, the wall
of chores, the grimy surfaces that obscure.
Go around the corners, under the broken fence,
crawl if you have to over moss, snail
slime, climb up the uneven hills
and down the dips through the snarl of vines
to the word pond with its scummy surface, frogs,
pond you found when you were seven,
and you slipped on mossy stones
and fell, breaking your birthday watch,
its yellow crystal, its bent and loosened black
Roman numerals, stopping time.
Pond you have had each time to refind,
kneel beside, brace yourself against
falling into, and reach into—fingers, wrist,
arm, shoulder—down, and down.

Crisis Clinic

My first night, a woman
    with her newborn in the sling
        of her arm listens from far off
to her voices. When her mother,
    who has brought her in, asks
        "Is the baby hungry?" she says,
    "I fed him yesterday."
When her mother says, "I think the baby is wet,"
    she answers, "I changed him yesterday."
    The techs and I go into the staff room.
I am the doctor. They say, "We're waiting
    for you to tell us what to do."

*

In the seclusion room,
    the man who dove onto the hood of the police car
        lies in restraints, loudly singing.
    Each time I pass, he calls, "Come lie down with me,"
        or "Bitch Doctor,"
    or "Please marry marry me."
By the front desk, a grieving mother,
    fluorescent lights. Yesterday her baby
        dragged a chair to a bureau, climbed
from chair onto bureau, bureau to ledge
    of the twenty-second-story window,
and fell. She wants
    Valium, she wants numbness.
My colleague, here to sign some charts,
    mutters, "Have her talk about it, instead."
    I stand, a locked door, between them.

*

In the upstairs On-Call Room,
    a narrow bed, bureau,
        vinyl-covered chair, unframed rectangle
    of mirror. It's 2 a.m.

34

I lie looking at shadows crouched
    on the ceiling. I wait
        for the bedside phone to ring.

*

The young woman whispers
        that ten days ago her husband
    moved them out here
            from Georgia. Then, last night, he left her
                in their one room with the babies,
    went up to the roof,
            and someone shot him,
                or he shot himself. The officer
    couldn't say. The officer told her
            to come here. She has no one, no money
                to bury him.
And how should she tell
        her five-, four-,
            and two-year-old children?
            I listen. I say
    that in the morning, when they open,
        I'll phone Family Crisis upstairs.
        I tell us both, "they can help."

*

3 a.m.: Stepping outside
    for air, I inhale fumes.
        The intersection
            of Sutter and Divisadero Streets glitters
    with broken glass. A drunk zigzags by,
        singing. The hospital security guard
    in the Emergency Room doorway
            hums off-key. The moonlight doesn't touch
                the grilled windows of the bank,
    the all-night convenience store.
        The moon fades over the city. It wants nothing
            to do with this.

*

The rookie policeman has brought in
        a girl-who-is-a-boy-who-is-a-girl
who is neither and nothing
        but insists, her hair wild,
    her jeans shredded. He lingers
        as I fill out the form
    that allows us to hospitalize her/him/her
        for 72 hours' surveillance, hot meals,
            a chance to talk and bathe.
My paperwork doesn't require him,
        but something slows his departure.
"Doc?" he says, "Oh, never mind."
        I sigh. He laughs.
"Me, too," he says, waves,
        leaves to return to his beat.

*

The young man sits wrapped
        in a blanket, still wet
    from his walk into the Pacific,
                still wondering why the woman
            walking on the beach
                walked into the ocean with him
    and when he changed his mind
        walked out with him
            and called the police.
We send for his deaf-mute father,
        his father's gay lover, his father's
            gay lover's neighbor
    who will translate sign.

I take a swallow of coffee; it's 4 a.m.
    I walk into the cubicle
        where they are gathered.
    Fluorescent light pours down
        on beige linoleum. Careful, I think.
            You could drown in there,
        all five
            on a broken raft.

36

*

For three hours, the boy in white
    has sat silent where the officer
      left him. He's answered
  no questions. He holds himself immobile,
      to outlast the voices.
   Periodically, I sit down
     beside him, talk a little: my name.
  Later, I say he looks frightened,
     maybe he took something or somebody gave him
 something and he's having a hard time.
     Later, that maybe he'd feel safer
        in the hospital. He nods,
    but slightly, trying not
      to fall off the ledge.

Now as I pass him,
    he glances almost at me,
      exhales a little.
  When the gurney comes, as I've told him
    it will, to take him to the ambulance,
  he whispers, looking just past me,
    "Tom," he says. "My name is Tom."

*

Hunched in the straight-backed chair,
    the man scowls. He's thin,
      about fifty. As I step towards him,
  he aims a metal ashtray to come close,
    but miss. It does. He freezes.
  I pick up the ashtray,
     put it on a nearby table, sit down
       three seats from him.
"Feel like talking?" I ask.
   He nods, puts his head in his hands, sobs.

*

This is the eleventh young gay-male-who-overdosed-
    when-his-lover-of-three-weeks-left-him
        that the techs have seen this week.
    Immune to their cynicism, he weeps
        as he sits in the interviewing cubicle,
            telling me his story. It's 5:30 in the morning.
I've heard this before. I know
        that after I hear about the short-term lover
            who left him, I'll ask gentle questions
        and there'll be a mother who died when he was three,
            a father who deserted—
    his first losses like fossils in rock.

*

    In the On-Call Room, the light
        has turned yellow.
            The glass over the bureau
        is chipped. I lie
rocking between caffeine
        and something-for-sleep.
Don't ring, I say aloud
        to the telephone. I have
    no answers, I can't
        answer, don't ring.

III.

Black Carp

Black carp of torn silk,
spilled ink in the water,
glimpsed, you swim
into memory, only you
from among the white,
the mottled orange,
the pale lemon splashed
with scarlet.

Glimpsed, you recur,
imposed on blanched faces, seen
on the gloss of the mahogany credenza,
the pale blue blush of plate.

Black carp of illusion, I hardly saw
your scales, fins, your
scalloped fan. Carp
of persistent echoing, only
your black shadow
in the green water.

You are someone held and lost,
and never held, urgent, remote.
He, the elusive shadow fish.
She, whose death the mind refuses.

Black of silence. The red anemone's
furled heart, the dilated pupil,
mourning ribbon, lost leather pencase.
Black of silk nightgowns,
and of the unutterable: VI, XII
of the clock face.

Black alone soothes
the hummingbird among blood drops
on hawthorns, leaves

loose rock beside the precipice,
a door held open.

Black carp seen in the pond
among the bright others,
you render them frivolous,
as the woman in black
does the woman in pink
at the party, the man
in the black suit all
of the others.

Los Feliz Hills

The old house sold now,
my nights northern
and companioned,
will I ever again,
in the dark,
the others
asleep, descend
the back stairs
with the worn
pomegranate runner,
open and slip out through
the sliding glass door,
feel the cool, rough nose
of the collie
on my palm, shed sandals, towel,
stand naked under the heavy-lidded eye
of the moon, the scent
of honeysuckle,
lemon, azalea, glide naked
into the pool, skin
slippery as the skin
of eggplant, plum, my body
scallop-white, turn
and pull effortlessly
through water, hear the dog
quietly panting the length
of the pool; pause, dive
towards the glitter
of the pool light,
come up into black,
turquoise, seeing wheels
of splintering ice?

Sweet Grapes, Cut

Having for the last time
seen the ocean, which
he always loved,
but which today he feared
to look at,
my father sits in the passenger seat
of his parked car, my husband
at the wheel, and I bring
my father chocolate yogurt,
his favorite treat,
in a fluted cup.
He eats in silence.
In a few weeks,
he will stop
eating.
He will tell me the remembered
beaches of my childhood had
metastatic riptides
and malignant bees.
He will try over and over, urgently,
to warn us about bridges.
Alone upstairs, he will fall and cry out.
I will run and find him
on his bedroom floor,
bewildered
and unable to rise. I will kneel beside him,
holding his hands. He will cry, "What
did I do to deserve this?"
Nothing, I will tell him.
He did nothing.
He is a good man, a good husband, a good
father. I will discover
what can be forgiven.
I will try to help him calm his fear,
as he helped me, sometimes.
I will sit and hear him say

that he has had enough
and do I know what he is asking.
When he hasn't peed all day,
all night, and still refuses water,
I will coax him
with sweet grapes cut
into quarters.
He will turn away.
None of this do I yet know
I know. I sit behind him
in the parked car,
our last outing.

Six Goodbyes

As he backs out of my driveway
on his way to the airport, he waves.
I don't show that his visit
has unraveled our old friendship.
Futile. Like trying to translate from Yiddish
that for which English has no equivalent.
I wave back.

*

My seventeen-year-old student
who, in ten minutes, will die on the freeway,
stands at my elbow waiting to speak.
I am engrossed with another; when I glance back
moments later, she is gone:
slim, fitted jeans,
pale blue turtleneck sweater,
blond hair wafting behind her,
long and newly washed.

*

I walk my friend to my door
and watch her walk
down the front path between wisteria
and flowering pear, under a shower of pollen
and a full moon.

I hear the engine of her car as she drives
down Zinn; the sound vanishes
before she reaches Snake Road.
What a good talk! Now the silence
enfolds her like a cape.

*

Tonight, after two years
of lullabyes and rocking,
lullabyes and rocking, suddenly
you are asleep by your own singing.
I wander our rooms in darkness.
Such sadness, and this
merely a rehearsal;
then, in an upstairs window,
the white November moon.

*

You respond to my invitation
with a few lines of which the letters
alternatingly spike and tremble like wet ink:

"I can no longer travel.
To your parents, and to you,
warmest regards."

*

She, who once flirted with the Nazi guards
and when they weren't looking,
threw parcels of medicine and food
over the barbed wire
into the ghetto of Warsaw,
raises her glass.
Here in the hospice,
we drink to the peonies and irises
hastily arranged on the table,
to the black-lacquered bowl
her husband brings her,
filled with plums and pears.

Yahrzeit

It seems I thought
you'd gone back to Los Angeles.
That I'd find you there
in your old office,
if only I returned. That
if I went to the beach
you always took us to,
the one in our home movies,
I would find you, resurrected
by the shore and sun. Instead,
my first trip here in years,
you're not with Mom
at the gate to pick me up.
Not at the reading,
where I so wanted you to be.
Not along these streets—
Wilshire, Sunset, Santa Monica—
streets whose names
you murmured like a lullaby,
streets that I was certain
you still drive among.
I keep thinking I'm about
to see you. You,
whom I can never
phone again to ask
which freeway I take
to find you. Which
offramp. You
who when my dog died
tried, but couldn't
make it clear to me
he wasn't coming home.

Wearing Away

Skiffs the tide carries to sea.
Stone steps worn bare by the soles'
erosion. The half life of friendships,
unpredictable.

I said (but it was the right thing to do).
I said (because of love, at the time). I said—
But she won't see you.

So many, the losses. Cumulative. Absence
of grains of sand, absence multiplied as absence,
so magnified that in time it grows visible.

On what planet of lost things will I find
the friends carried off
in the ship divorce? In the boat death?
In the bus another place? In the swerve

of a truth told that perhaps
shouldn't have been? In the quarrel
that expanded?

In the turn time takes
unexpectedly because a tree has fallen,
blocking the road?

Prayer: Hoh Rainforest

Dwarfed, we stand at the roots of cedar, hemlock,
spruce, peer up and up: moss the gray-green of jasper
trails from the high branches. Light pierces—
spears of it, arrows. Further on, the stream,
clear to its bottom, two fish like lucid thoughts,
and a coin, half buried. I look into the water,
try to listen, but my son, who had wandered ahead,
comes back, chatters, drums on my ear, shatters
cadences, pierces the veils
of gray, the timber altars, benches.
Quiet, I say, please,
but still he chatters as we pass white fungi like hurled discuses
embedded in spruce, fallen cross-sections, like sculpture,
of red and gold rainforest cedar. We study a bug,
sheer-winged and green as snow peas. I want to trace
the gossamer frets of those wings. But my boy chatters
like seven monkeys, swears, banters. I beg him
for silence, the silence of clear forest brook,
of ferns—sword fern and bracken, licorice ferns
growing up from the limbs
of maples, silence of nurse logs vanished,
in a mere century, after saplings of sitka spruce
and hemlock grew up out of them to tower, tower,
rooted now in nothing
visible, roots rounding and looped
over nothing. I beg but my child jabbers, leaps—bats
sweeping through hushed cathedrals, candles
tumble, chalices overturn. I hiss, then shriek
at him to stop, please, just
for a heartbeat, here where a single log, if hollowed,
could house us, where flowers on the forest floor
resemble strewn stars, where a saber-toothed tiger
between tree trunks wouldn't surprise me,
or a gilded stag with a trumpet. But
the child recites limericks, mimics
banshees, drives off the silence
that I long to enter and vanish into. . . .

I listen for you, silence,
in the fish-skeleton and quill shapes
of these fern fronds,
in the capes and torn curtains of moss, in the brown
monks' robes of the mushrooms, in the brook
with its fish circling, in fallen logs.
I listen for you.

Voices, After the Firestorm

        fire, I am calm, calm, bursts
            the parched eucalyptus, incandescent bark,
        shrapnel of branch, gas tanks explode,
houses, leaves only foundations, leaps the six-lane highway
            I am placid, your words
        did not offend me, all
but the asphalt evaporated, neighborhoods
        turned to ash, a ceramic mug, I am serene,
            nothing would make me shriek, I feel nothing, my house
        didn't, not mine, gates writhe, thousands
        of gates, houses, twenty-five bodies,
            their lungs smoke, their flesh blackened.

*

It burned in four minutes. Not
one wall left, not one.

*

Listen to   them   city   people   shocked
by fire   claiming arson
or negligence   as if to blame
gives us control back   halts
what we can't harness   They don't   know fire
how   Listen
how they pretend if we are careful
pretend   as if anyone
could have saved us   as if she could have saved me
as if the flames   his hands   mouth   the rest
that scorched   me   could
have been prevented   had I dared
blame or protest   blame   could he then
have been stopped
had she   been careful   watched
seen and doused those first
small fires?

*

It isn't the houses for me. Or the lives.
    It's the fire in the cemetery, fire
        over graves, fire I know he came back
            from the dead and started, to punish. Anger—
            and the trees over the buried, burned, and ash
    on the graves. This is wrong of me, to grieve
        for the trees, for grass over the dead, for the terror
        he must have felt, new
            to his coffin, hearing the crackling
        the roar my fury. How dare I
    blame him for leaving us?

*

It's not like you see the unfaded rectangle
on the wall where the picture was
and miss the picture.   Because there is
no longer the wall.   Or the room. No
picture; no place on which to hang

*

She is the arsonist—*she*, the fire
the wind unleashed—*she*—
who drops her lit cigarettes
in dry weeds—her vitriol—indifferent
to book manuscripts, paintings,
to photographs—to the index cards—
the research notes painstakingly gathered—
a life—she can't see what that means—
can't—Sees only what is hers—
Like her—Can't see me—
or what these hills were—
she who is oblivious—
to rooms lovingly furnished—
who eats house after house,
incinerating menwomenchildren trying to flee—

she whose lusts are kindling enough—
whose fury tinder enough—
to do to these hills as to me.

*

I made myself known, I
who should have kept
silent. Don't stand out
they always said, who
do you think you are,
they always said, I spoke
before all
of those people,
won their respect,
held their attention,
and look: houses
melted, ridges
like charred meat,
people homeless, people
killed in their cars,
their driveways. I
didn't do this, I know I
have nothing
to do with this,
I belong
sealed up.

*

After abstinence,
we two fierce,
October fierce, wind
a sirocco, an onrushing
tiger, fur, teeth,
long drought
having turned hillsides
to tinder, each stalk
a mute force
awaiting release, each

limb ready. Our first
sparks: torches
of eucalyptus, pyres
of pine, kindling of grass,
of houses, neighborhoods. Jets
of fire, walled cities
of fire,
purgatory, ecstatic.

*

I stood on our roof, watching
the fire come, stood and screamed at the wind,
wind blowing towards us, orange and black mountain
of fire, stood and screamed at the wind, black smoke
and a vortex, leaping nearer, screamed at the wind
get down, I told myself, screamed at the wind, get down,
get your things, her things, the briefcases, baby pictures,
get the pets, get down, get out, it's coming, screamed,
screaming won't stop it—is screaming what stopped it?
stopped it just here?—stood on the roof, hosing the roof,
screamed Turn away, Turn away, at the wind.

*

Ash, and acrid air. The chimneys twisted, charred
memorials. We pick like birds among the ruins.
A baby's drinking cup. A finial from a lamp.
A photo, its edges singed, curled.
We don't suspect the griefs that await.
Nor what is dormant, under the blackened earth.

About the Author

Susan Kolodny's poems appear in several literary journals including *New England Review* and *Beloit Poetry Journal*, and in several anthologies, most recently *The Place That Inhabits Us—Poems of the San Francisco Bay Watershed* (16 Rivers, 2010). She received her MFA in Poetry from the Program for Writers at Warren Wilson College. A former college English teacher, she is a psychoanalyst and psychotherapist practicing in Oakland, where she specializes in work with artists and writers. She teaches at the San Francisco Center for Psychoanalysis, where she founded and chairs an event series called Poetry & Psychoanalysis. She is the author of *The Captive Muse: On Creativity and Its Inhibition* (PsychoSocial Press, 2000). *After the Firestorm* (Mayapple Press, 2011) is her first poetry collection.

Other Recent Titles from Mayapple Press:

Eleanor Lerman, *Janet Planet*, 2011
        Paper, 210pp, $16.95 plus s&h
        ISBN 978-1-936419-06-7
George Dila, *Nothing More to Tell*, 2011
        Paper, 100pp, $15.95 plus s&h
        ISBN 978-1-936419-05-0
Sophia Rivkin, *Naked Woman Listening at the Keyhole*, 2011
        Paper, 44pp, $13.95 plus s&h
        ISBN 978-1-936419-04-3
Stacie Leatherman, *Stranger Air*, 2011
        Paper, 80pp, $14.95 plus s&h
        ISBN 978-1-936419-03-6
Mary Winegarden, *The Translator's Sister*, 2011
        Paper, 86pp, $14.95 plus s&h
        ISBN 978-1-936419-02-9
Howard Schwartz, *Breathing in the Dark*, 2011
        Paper, 96pp, $15.95 (hardcover $24.95) plus s&h
        ISBN 978-1-936419-00-5 (hc 978-1-936419-01-2)
Paul Dickey, *They Say This Is How Death Came into the World*, 2011
        Paper, 78 pp, $14.95 plus s&h
        ISBN 978-0932412-997
Sally Rosen Kindred, *No Eden*, 2011
        Paper, 70 pp, $14.95 plus s&h
        ISBN 978-0932412-980
Jane O. Wayne, *The Other Place You Live*, 2010
        Paper, 80 pp, $14.95 plus s&h
        ISBN 978-0932412-973
Andrei Guruianu, *Metal and Plum: A Memoir*, 2010
        Paper, 124 pp, $16.95 plus s&h
        ISBN 978-0932412-966
Jeanne Larsen, *Why We Make Gardens (& Other Poems)*, 2010
        Paper, 74 pp, $14.95 plus s&h
        ISBN 978-0932412-959
Jayne Pupek, *The Livelihood of Crows*, 2010
        Paper, 86 pp, $15.95 plus s&h
        ISBN 978-0932412-942

For a complete catalog of Mayapple Press publications, please visit our website at *www.mayapplepress.com*. Books can be ordered direct from our website with secure on-line payment using PayPal, or by mail (check or money order). Or order through your local bookseller.